HAL•LEONARD®

DRUM PLAY-ALONG

AUDIO ACCESS INCLUDED

VOL. 9

COVER BAND HITS

PLAYBACK+
Speed • Pitch • Balance • Loop

To access audio visit:
www.halleonard.com/mylibrary

Enter Code
2029-3402-5372-3674

ISBN 978-1-4950-8558-1

HAL•LEONARD®

7777 W. BLUEMOUND RD. P.O. BOX 13819 MILWAUKEE, WI 53213

Visit Hal Leonard Online at
www.halleonard.com

CONTENTS

Cruise

Words and Music by Chase Rice, Tyler Hubbard,
Brian Kelley, Joey Moi and Jesse Rice

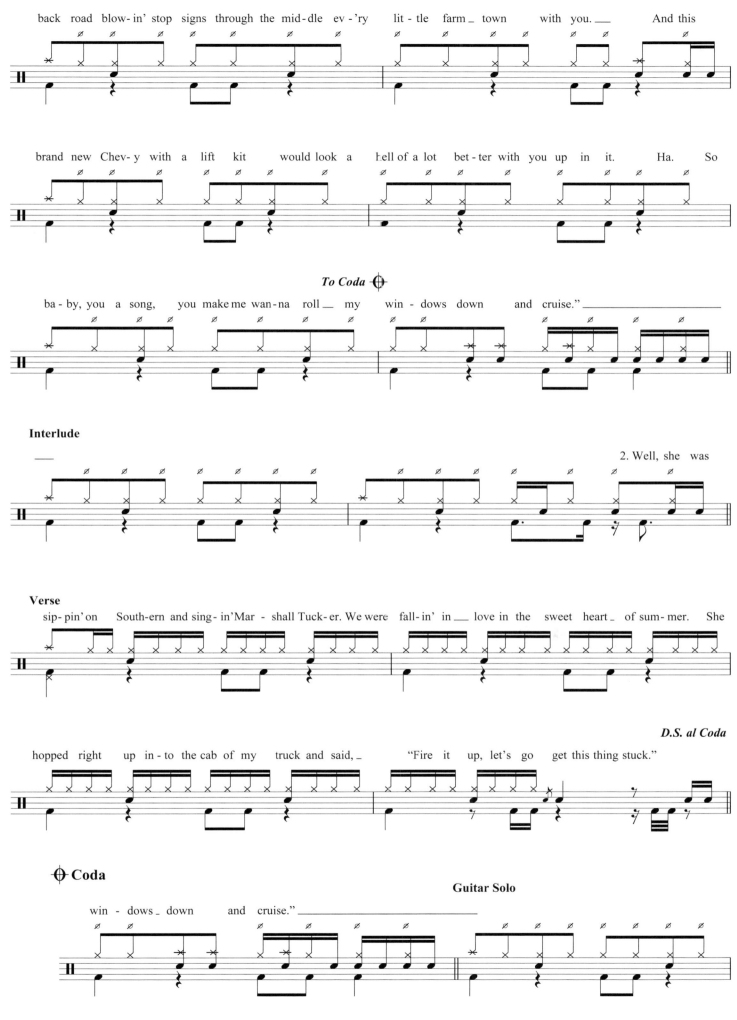

Bridge

When that _____ sum - mer sun fell to his knees _ I _____

_____ looked at her and she _ looked at me. Then I turned on those _ K - C lights and drove _

_____ all night 'cause it felt so right, her _ and I, _ man, we felt _ so right. 3. I

Verse

put it in _____ park and grab _ my gui - tar and strum _ a cou - ple chords and sang _ from the heart.

Girl, you sure _ got the beat in my chest bump - in'. Hell, I can't get you out of my head. _____

Chorus

Ba - by, you a song, you make me wan - na roll _ my win - dows _ down and cruise. _ Down a

back road blow-in' stop signs through the mid-dle ev-'ry lit-tle farm_ town with you. ____ Well,

ba-by, you a song, you make me wan-na roll__ my win-dows_ down and cruise._ Down a

back road blow-in' stop signs through the mid-dle ev-'ry lit-tle farm_ town with you._ And this

brand new Chev-y with a lift kit would look a hell of a lot bet-ter with you up in it. C'-mon.

Ba-by, you a song, you make me wan-na roll__ my win-dows down and cruise. ____

Outro

____ C'-mon, girl. ____ Get those win-dows down_ and cruise._

____ Ah, ____ yeah. ____

back road blow-in' stop signs through the mid-dle ev-'ry lit-tle farm_ town

Ex's & Oh's

Words and Music by Tanner Schneider and Dave Bassett

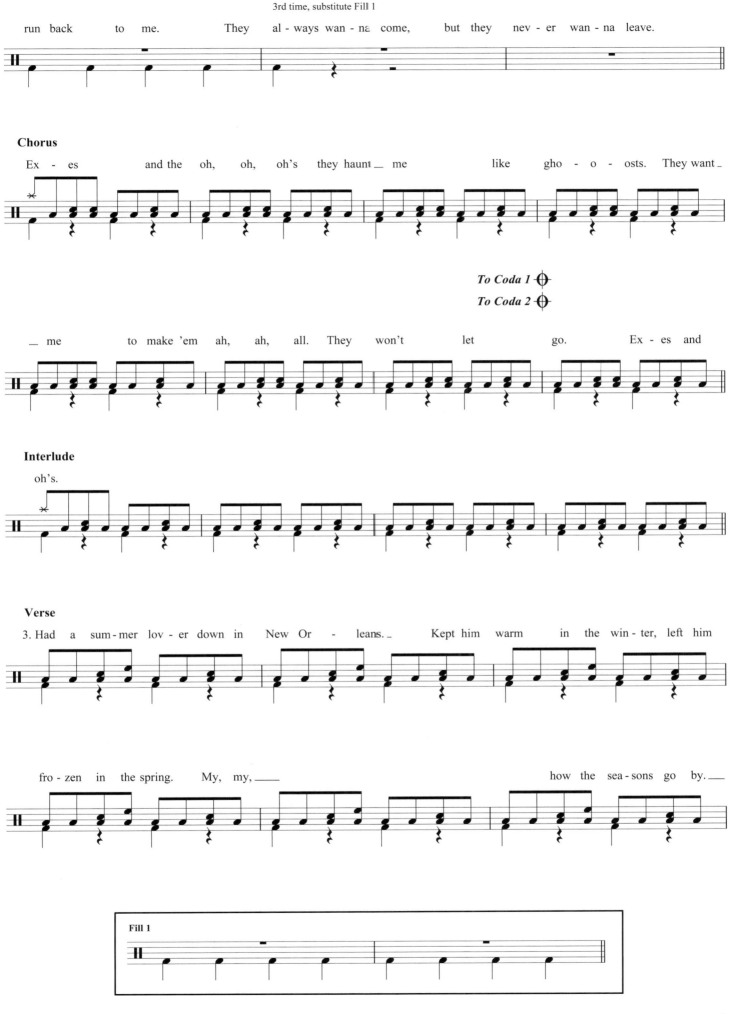

run back to me. They al - ways wan - na come, but they nev - er wan - na leave.

Chorus

Ex - es and the oh, oh, oh's they haunt ___ me like gho - o - osts. They want ___

To Coda 1

To Coda 2

___ me to make 'em ah, ah, all. They won't let go. Ex - es and

Interlude

oh's.

Verse

3. Had a sum - mer lov - er down in New Or - leans. ___ Kept him warm in the win - ter, left him

fro - zen in the spring. My, my, ___ how the sea - sons go by. ___

Fill 1

Verse

4. I get high, ___ and I love to get low, ___ so the hearts keep break-ing and the heads just roll. ___ You know, ___ ___ that's how the sto - ry goes. ___

D.S. al Coda 1

Coda 1

go. My ex - es ___ and the oh, oh, oh's they haunt ___ me like gho - o - osts. They want ___ ___ me to make 'em ah, ah, all. They won't let

Guitar Solo

go. Ex - es and oh's.

D.S. al Coda 2

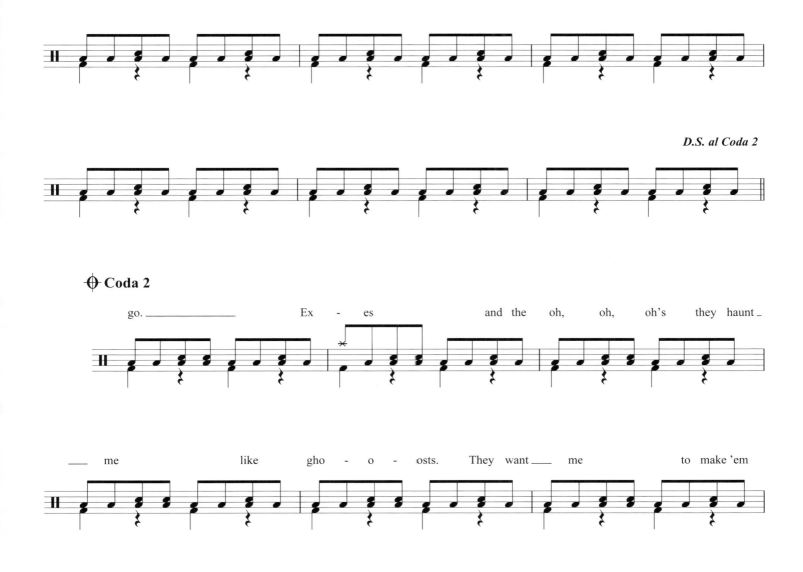

Ⓞ **Coda 2**

go. _____ Ex - es and the oh, oh, oh's they haunt_

___ me like gho - o - osts. They want___ me to make 'em

ah, ah, all. They won't let go. Ex - es and

Outro

oh's.

Additional Lyrics

2. Now, there's one in California who's been cursing my name,
   'Cause I found me a better lover in the U.K.
   Hey, hey, until I made my getaway.

Pre-Chorus 3. One, two, three, they gonna run back to me,
   Climbing over mountains and, uh, sailing over seas.
   One, two, three, they gonna run back to me.
   They always wanna come, but they never wanna leave.

Get Lucky

Words and Music by Thomas Bangalter,
Guy Manuel Homem Christo, Nile Rodgers and Pharrell Williams

Intro
Moderately ♩ = 116

1. Like the leg-end of __ the phoe-

%‌ Verse

- nix,   huh,   all ends __ with __ be - gin - nings.
2. *See additional lyrics*

What keeps the plan - et spin - ning,   ah, _____ the force from the __ be - gin-

Pre-Chorus

- ning,   look.   We've   come too far __

to give up _____   who we are. _____   So,

let's   raise the bar _____   and our cups _____   to the stars. __

To Coda ⊕

Chorus

__   She's up __ all   night __ till the sun,   I'm up __ all   night __ to get some.

She's up __ all   night _ for good fun,   I'm up __ all   night _ to get _ luck - y.   We're up __ all   night _ till the sun,

we're up __ all   night _ to get some.   We're up __ all   night _ for good fun,   we're up __ all   night _ to get luck - y.

We're up __ all   night _ to get luck-y.   We're up __ all   night _ to get luck-y.   We're up __ all   night _ to get luck-y.

Interlude

We're up __ all   night _ to   get _ luck - y.

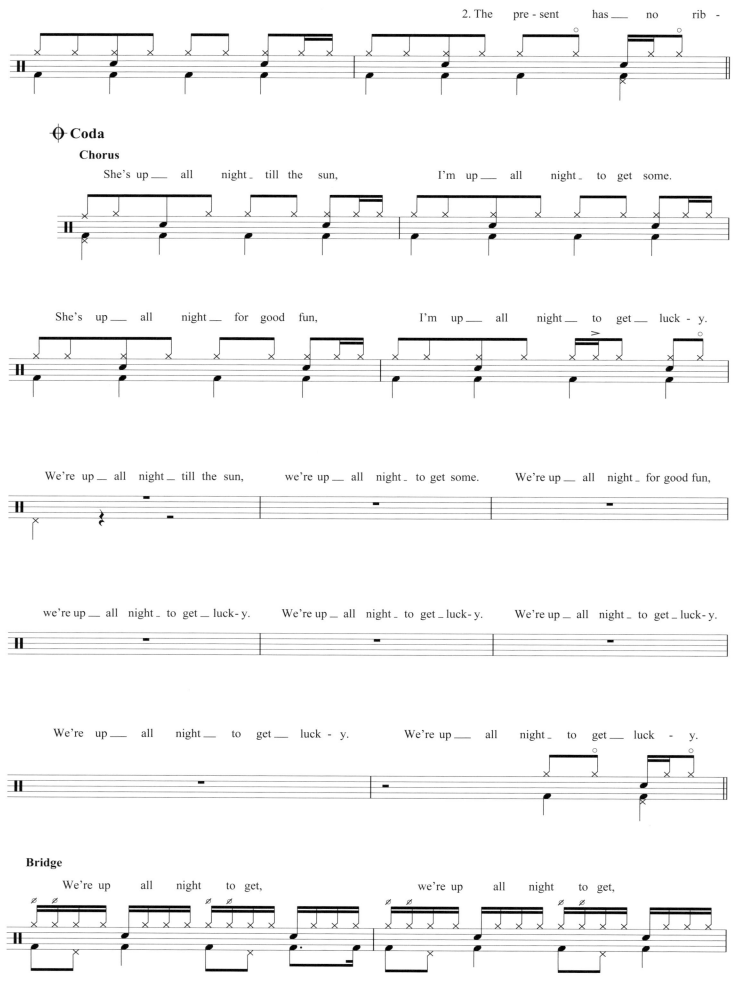

Coda

Chorus

Bridge

we're up   all   night   to get,   we're up   all   night   to get.

We're up   all   night   to get,   we're up   all   night   to get,

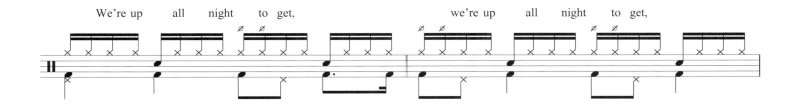

we're up   all   night   to get,   we're up   all   night   to get.

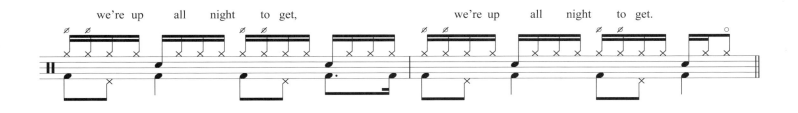

We're up   all   night_ to get   luck - y.   We're up   all   night_ to get   luck - y.

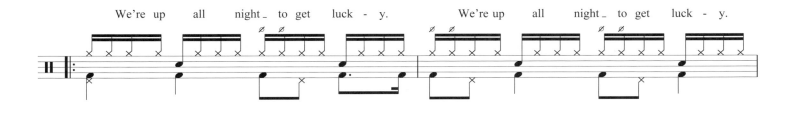

We're up   all   night_ to get   luck - y.   We're up   all   night_ to get   luck - y.

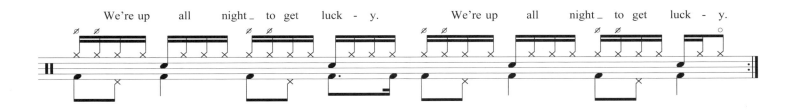

Pre-Chorus

We've   come   too   far_____   to   give   up_____

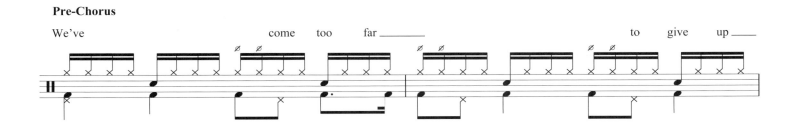

_   who   we   are._____   So,

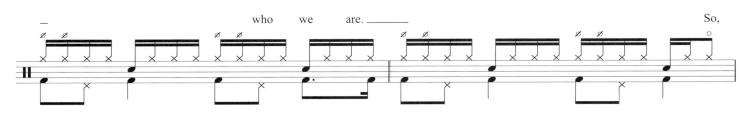

let's   raise   the   bar _____   and   our   cups __

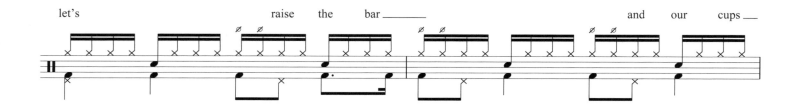

__   to   the   stars. _____

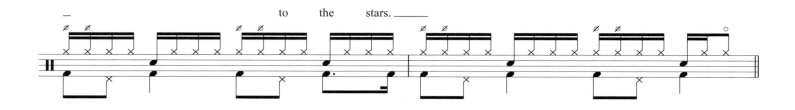

Chorus

She's up __ all   night _ till the   sun,   I'm up __ all   night _ to get   some.

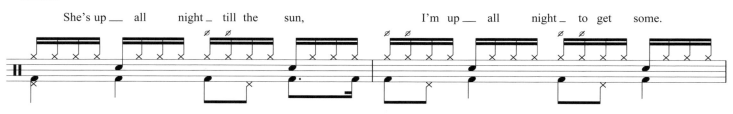

She's up __ all   night _ for good   fun,   I'm up __ all   night _ to get _ luck - y.

We're up __ all   night _ till the   sun,   we're up __ all   night _ to get   some.

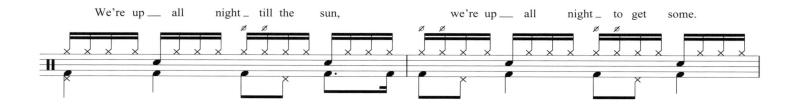

We're up __ all   night _ for good   fun,   we're up __ all   night _ to get _ luck - y.

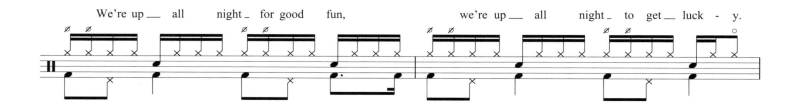

We're up __ all   night _ to get _ luck - y.   We're up __ all   night _ to get _ luck - y.

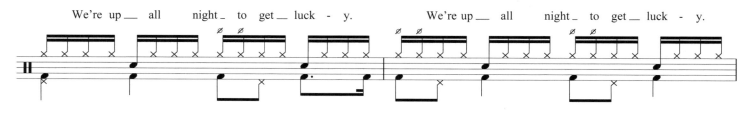

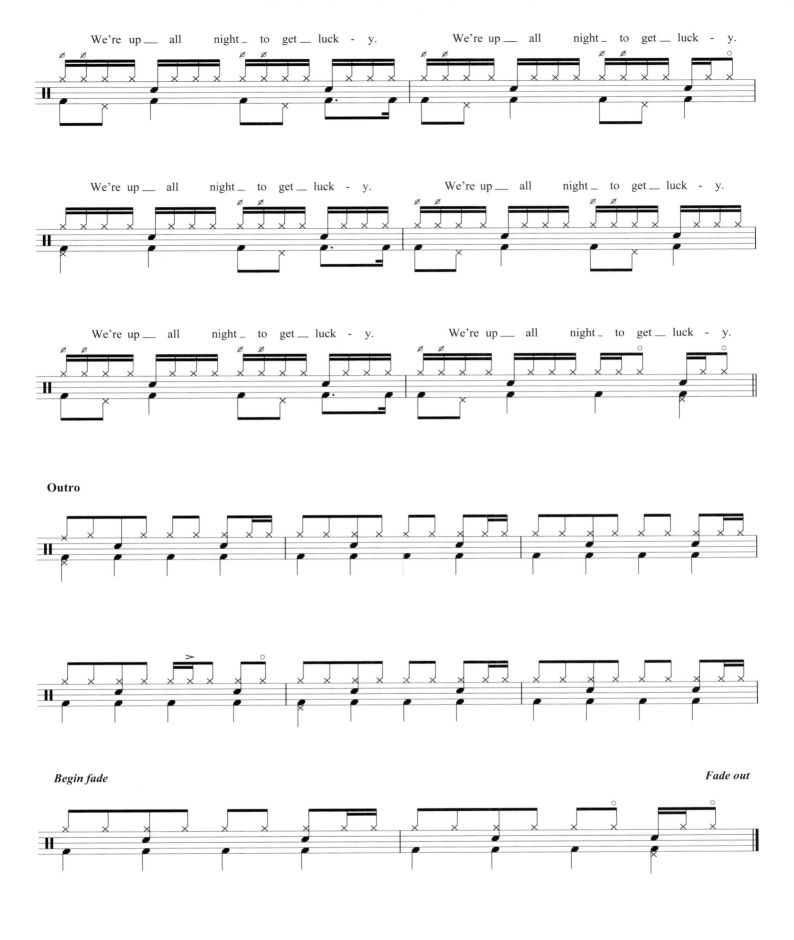

Additional Lyrics

2. The present has no ribbon,
   Your gift keeps on giving.
   What is this I'm feeling?
   If you wanna leave, I'm ready, ah.

Nobody to Blame

Words and Music by Chris Stapleton, Ronnie Bowman
and Barry Bales

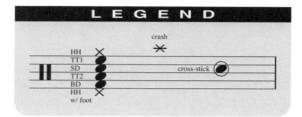

I got no - bod - y to blame _____ but

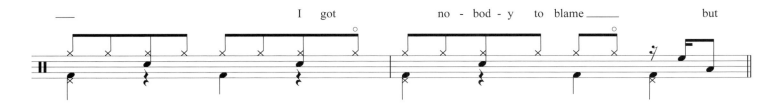

Outro

me. __

Begin fade

Fade out

21

Thinking Out Loud

Words and Music by Ed Sheeran and Amy Wadge

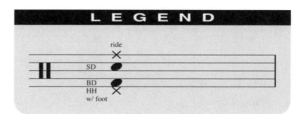

Verse
Moderately slow ♩ = 79

1. When your legs don't work like they used to be - fore ___

and I can't sweep you off of your feet.

Will your mouth still re - mem - ber the taste of my love?

Will your eyes still smile ___ from your cheeks? And dar - ling, I ___

%

___ will ___ be lov - ing you 'til ___ we're sev - en - ty. ___

3. *See additional lyrics*

*Wire brushes on ride, drumstick on snare.

And ba - by, my ___

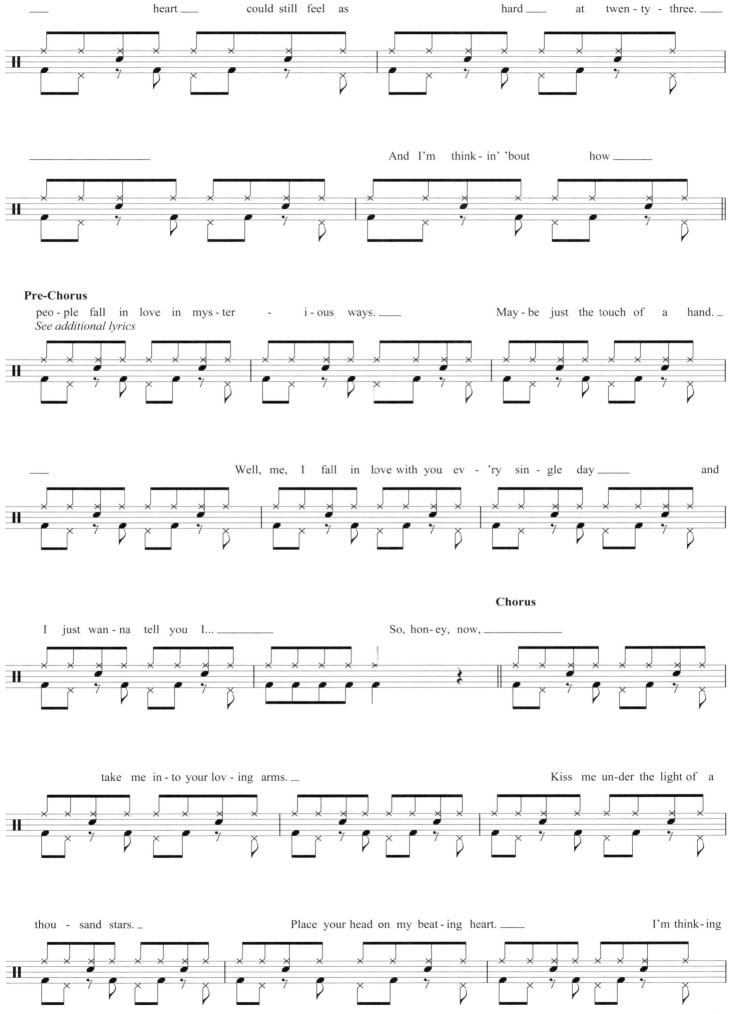

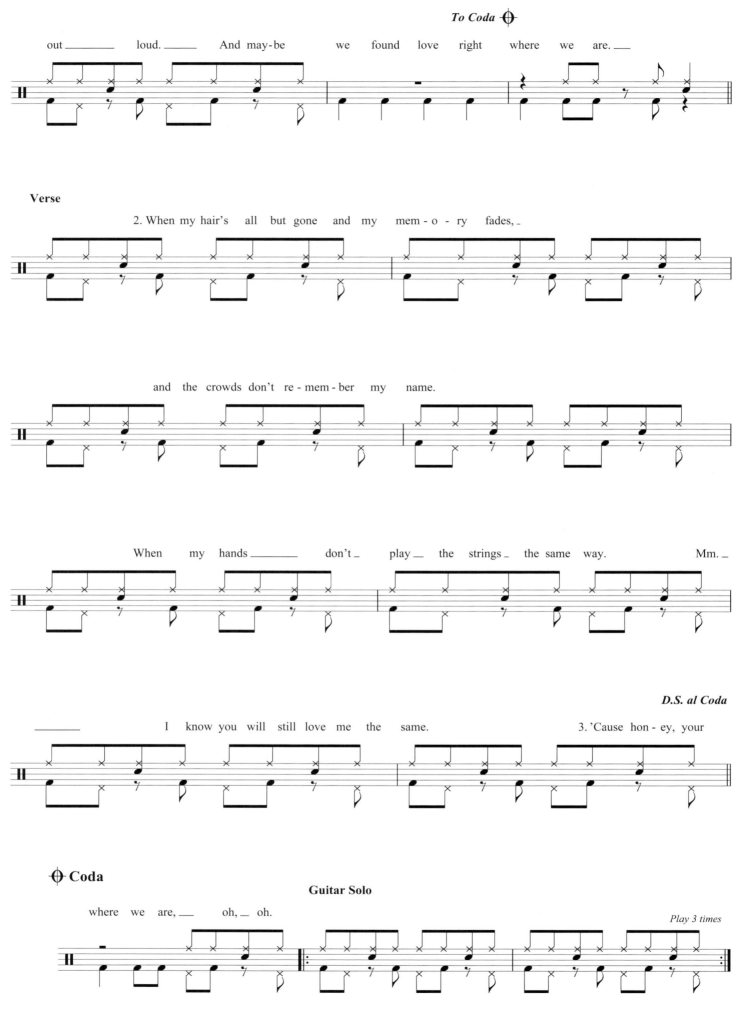

Additional Lyrics

3. 'Cause honey, your soul could never grow old, it's evergreen.
And baby, your smile's forever in my mind and memory.

Pre-Chorus I'm thinkin' 'bout how people fall in love in mysterious ways
And maybe it's all part of a plan.
Well, I'll just keep on making the same mistakes;
Hoping that you'll understand. That baby, now...

Shut Up and Dance

Words and Music by Ryan McMahon, Ben Berger, Sean Waugaman,
Eli Maiman, Nicholas Petricca and Kevin Ray

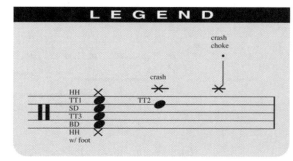

Intro

Moderately fast ♩ = 128

Pre-Chorus

D.S. al Coda

Coda

Synth Solo

Chorus

dare look back, just keep your eyes on __ me." I said, "You're hold - in' __ back." She said, "Shut

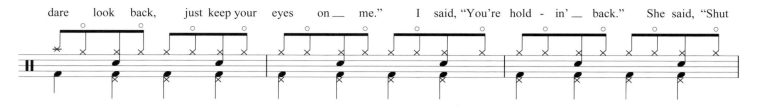

up and dance with me." This wom - an is my des - ti - ny. She said,

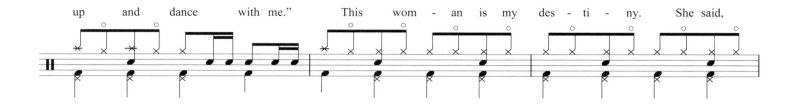

"Oo, _____ hoo. __ Shut up and dance with me. _____

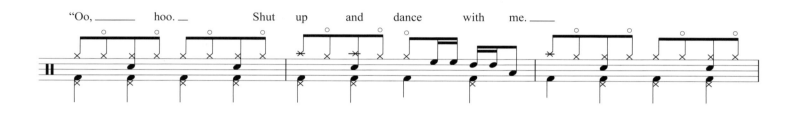

Oo, _____ hoo. __ Shut up and dance with me. __

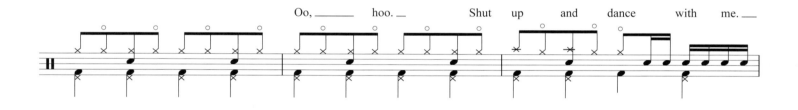

__ Oo, _____ hoo. __ Shut

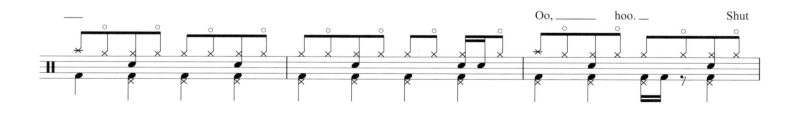

up and dance with me." ___

Uptown Funk

Words and Music by Mark Ronson, Bruno Mars, Philip Lawrence,
Jeff Bhasker, Devon Gallaspy, Nicholaus Williams, Lonnie Simmons,
Ronnie Wilson, Charles Wilson, Rudolph Taylor and Robert Wilson

Chucks on ___ with Saint Lau - rent. ___ Got - ta kiss my - self, ___ I'm so pret - ty. I'm too

Pre-Chorus

hot, (Hot damn!) call the po - lice ___ and the fire - man. I'm too hot, (Hot damn!) make a

drag - on wan - na re - tire, ___ man. ___ I'm too hot, (Hot damn!) Say my name, ___ you know who I am. ___ I'm too

hot. (Hot damn!) Am I bad 'bout ___ that mon - ey? Break it down.

Chorus

Girls hit ___ you, hal - le - lu - jah. Girls hit ___ you, hal - le - lu - jah. Girls hit ___ you, hal - le - lu - jah. 'Cause

up - town funk gon' give it to ya. 'Cause up - town funk gon' give it to ya.

Sat - ur - day night ___ and we in the spot. ___ Don't be - lieve ___ me? Just watch. Come on!

Bridge

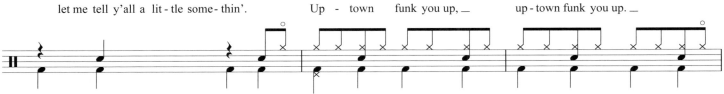

Additional Lyrics

2. Stop! Wait a minute.
Fill my cup, put some liquor in it.
Take a sip, sign the check.
Julio, get the stretch.
Ride to Harlem, Hollywood,
Jackson, Mississippi.
If we show up, we gon' show out.
Smoother than a fresh jar of Skippy.

The Walker

Words and Music by Michael Fitzpatrick, Jeremy Ruzumna,
Noelle Scaggs, Joseph Karnes, James Midhi King
and John Meredith Wicks

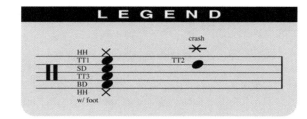

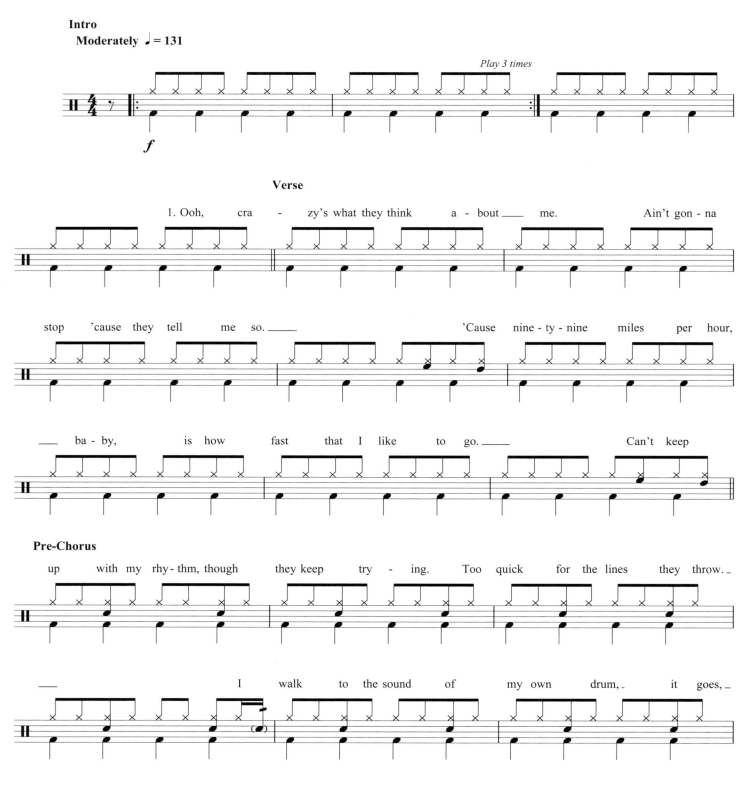

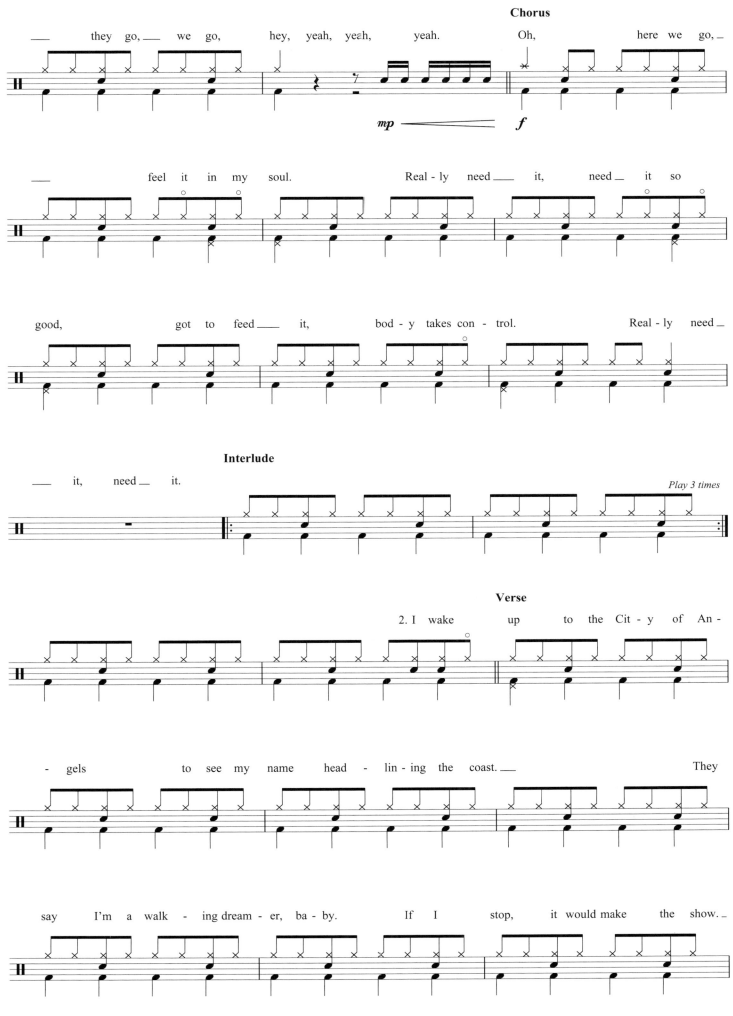

Chorus